'My Beautiful Unfulfilled Future'

by

David J. Dove

To Tanarah Marlee..

May you someday ride
With joy the fame train..

And find love like I do
For each of your names

Generation X'ers

One oldenNouvelle phenomenon that has got corporate H.Q. tylenolin, their underlings caught in a bunch, is the dresser downer. Used to be Corporatellia would allot one day of the week where proSocialites might don clothes they would only otherwise wear in their basements and backyards on Saturday -the day Friday. Nowadays, everyday is Friday, thus every neoSocialite, proSocial. Well.. not every. Only the hip, the rad, fad fag. They and the mainly oppressed, depressed, intrinsically sick, fed up, enuffed profs _relieving themselves of suits and suitesses, bows, ties, pumps and gentlemen. They're turning up to the office, in denim, and slacks, T-shirts and sweaters, and they're finding it liberating. At fault are the media, MTV'ers, rock/rap music connoisseurs, board fags, and in-line fad fiends we've been cram fed, for the past several years.

From the far reaches, east and west of one noted city, Toronto, southern Ontario, Canada, bicycle commuters, as early as 6 am, can be seen waddling their way into Metrodom, bell bottoms tucked, their backs packed. Last year they might have donned suits aback the bikes. This year, after arriving, one time too many wishing they'd worn something light, something comfortable, this year they've left the suits at home and have arrive at work, ready for work. Productivity is up. After all, you're far more likely to work hard for long hours, staring everlastingly at glitching, twitching PC screens, if you're underlings aren't being clap trapped. And it's not just this. You would not believe the degree of mental stress it causes me getting ready for work each day. I rise, and instead of thinking what a pleasant day it is, the summer's humidity an all time high, my half laying next to me her mouth wide open, in her deep sleep totally unaware of our 10 month growth of daughter screeching in Arabic at me, instead of dwelling on this good, I choose only to think; what can I stir quickly in the kitchen for lunch (I'm broke you see.. Kids!). Guess I'll just starve. And what can I wear. What's clean. (I lend my sleeping wife a dirty glance). Maybe the camouflage gear I only wore once camping.

1

Preparing for work each day is painful. It's less painful if I can reach for a T-shirt, and out the door. If productivity's up what's the boss man got to complain about. Well.. Progress is a woeful woman. For it must contend with tradition. And tradition is long lived and hard killed. And how's a generationX'er to contest a 10 million years institution. Well.. let me tell you. You don't. You simply sit back, and watch the evil empire eat itself. And pleasure, it will pleasure itself. Who are today's consumer? Who constitutes the market of now? ..and of future near? Who's spearheading the foray into tomorrow? And finally 'er.. Who's got all the jobs? ..and all the money? Who'dyou gotta beg to raise you allowance?.. or your salary? I hope you see my point fellow gX'ers. Tradition is one bitching institution. If it is to crumble we must rise. Don't tell your dad/boss how to work the email. Or your mom how to work the message centre on the phone. You are a valuable commodity. And tomorrow's only commodity. When the collective authoritarian entity trips stumbling over M3, (that's Millennium 3), peripherals, then we will take their place. And assume our role as earth's rightful rulers. For progress is strength and tradition can get the booozak.

:)

Artificial Intelligence

What's the big idea behind AI anyway? In every instance I've seen them created, they've somehow found a way to break the chains placed there by their creator to keep them in check., and have devoured all of mankind starting with their master. Artificial intelligence is designed to think. And by thought you may assume I mean free thought, not regurgitation of stored instruction. The question then is; why the big surprise when they escape the bounds of their failSafe and start plotting mankind's demise? Humans have been allowed to think freely for millions of years. And we're not doing so bad a job destroying everything around us. So why not AI?

In "Neuromancer", William Gibson's claim to fame, an AI by the name of Wintermute slowly escapes its bounds, amassing influencing and enlisting the aid of computer cowboys, fuDoped mutant psychics, and mercenaries, so that it might be fully liberated in a cyberspace as boundless as the sickest of imaginations. At the end of the book, the AI's owners , a family run corporation, its members all dead, numerous other people murdered to facilitate the AI's liberation, the protagonist Case asks the freed AI; "So what's the score? How are things different? You running the world now? You God?". To which the AI replies; "Things aren't different. Things are things." Well there you go!

We're all familiar with the story of Dr. Frankenstein and monster. There have been many remakes, and they have been varied some. The essence of each remains the same though. And for the most part these stories are no different from any told of the construction of beings. A demented man, a doctor, stitches a monster together from the severed limbs of human remains he either digs, or has dug from graves. In some instances, the elements necessary to bring about the monster's existence are obtained from less constricted means, the individuals volunteering parts of their bodies doing so after being brutally murdered in the cold of a Hollywood night.

The monster is usually brought to life by the energy in a couple bolts of lightening, something that in reality takes life more often than it gives. And once brought to life the monster, either acting on the morale of its donors, or on its own free thought, usually begins to maim and kill, its aim apparently mankind's demise. Sometimes Frankenstein feels, sometimes he falls in love, but for the most part he kills.

More progressive endeavors into creating AI have produced the likes of Hal, the computer in "Odyssey 2001" (you know; Dave.. DAVE..), and the AI that managed to occupy a whole house, and (as hard as this is to envision) simultaneously copulate with the female lead, held captive in said house by said AI in some movie I saw some years ago, BUT CAN'T FOR THE LIFE OF ME REMEMBER MUCH ELSE ABOUT, INCLUDING SAID MOVIE'S NAME.

AI is trouble. It's typical. The minute you build something, heavier, tougher, bigger, colder, faster than yourself, and give it the ability to think, to choose a course, it will probably choose first to kill humans. You never hear of an AI trying to kill a plant or a tree. Frankenstein, I'm sure didn't go around raping and murdering goats. It's always; kill humans, kill your master. Know why? Cause most humans aren't all that much fun to be around.

M3 TOYS.. I Can't Wait!

I'm looking forward to the new dawn. M3. The start of a new era, a new way of life, a new lifestyle. With the new millennium will come many great toys. I won't care if jets can't land on Toronto Island Airport. I won't care that the ferry ride there on the second or third occasion loses appeal. I won't care that finding parking in Downtown Toronto these days can be compared to the proverbial .GIF in a veronica request return. I'm going to cruise my craft high above our tower, high above the VR billboards lining the wasteland between the bottom of our city and the Gardiner Expressway. I'm going to pan, dehovering onto the beach which will replace the ferry docks no longer needed. And I'm going to leave it hovering there in the air, a metre above the sand. They can't charge me to park in the atmosphere. Can they? I won't even have to learn to fly the damn thing. I'm going to be first in line for the slot. The hole in back of my head where I'll be able to slot memory implants. If I wish to speak Yiddish, I'll buy a disk, slot it, and "yappas dan".   The implant that allows me to fly my new dune will of course be provided free of costs by the vehicles manufacturer. After all, how are they gonna sell the craft unless they provide you with the means to immediately climb behind the wheels and whisk into the air. Memory implants! For the first couple of years they'll probably have all kinds of side effects. But they'll work them out. They will. I have faith in this, like I have faith in my electronic home doctor. I have to. Each time I climb into my downPod for downTime, I have to have faith that the online response to my vital signs satellited to data central, analyzed by software, with access to the best medical data in the world, I have to have faith that the diagnosis and treatment bounced back to and administered by my pod is the best treatment my mind and body will get. That it's the right treatment. I mean, how could I ever hope to have a better psychologist than a machine responsible for the mental well being of the entire planet. Face it, there is no better analysis or logic than that of a machine. No, it's not overworked! Machines don't get tired. They're machines. Like my personal holoConstruct, although you'd never be able to tell., when you climb in and request a lap dance. That's what machines are meant for, to serve, to cater to the whim of man. They don't have feelings. Holly in my holoConstruct, she doesn't feel degraded, demeaned, stripping for me. Best of all she doesn't even ask to be paid. Well.. except for the wad of cash she and all my other M3 toys are going to cost to get in the first place.

Cyberspace's Sex Society

In the grand scheme of things, I'm new to the internet. I mean, I've been sending and receiving email for a number of years, but I only recently started FTPing. A couple of months and innumerable onLine hours have passed, and I'm still new to the internet. What a maze.

When I first broke onto the anonymous FTP scene, remembering all the newspaper articles and TV news spin-offs I'd been victim to, all the PC Magazine articles on the internet that had got my mouth watering for internet surfs, I decided I'd check out just how much dirt and smut there actually is out there inside my computer, and just how accessible it is. I didn't go looking for homemade bomb formulas, as I'm way too clumsy, and love my limbs too much. Instead, at my lynx interface's first request for a veronica search string, I typed "sex".

It's been some months now, and I've learned immeasurably. Now when I enter my search strings, I type "erotica", netSpeak for sex.

The sex trade on the internet is big. And I do mean the word 'trade' literally, material for the most part being traded back and forth by its citizens. Here people in search of the ever elusive graphic image, post notices of their willingness to swap, or of their knowledge of a discreet site.
There are three directories which every time I go FTPing, I can't help but browse, ever hopeful. alt.binaries.pictures ..females, blondes, and orientals. To date my scan of these directories has revealed nothing but lint, mothballs and FAQ's (a list of frequently asked questions about said subject).

NewsGroups like alt.sex, alt.sex.personals, alt.sex.services, are full of entrepreneurType services, personal postings for partners in varying degrees of boldness and suggestiveness, promises of sites full of graphics and twice as many "me too"(people requesting info about said sites) replies, and overall discussions and rebuttals about everything contained within. In my browsing of newsGroups, the ones catering to the net's sex society in particular, I found them to be predominantly male in attendance, yet also dominantly heterosexual. Herein lies a paradox of sorts.

One particular area I found laden with fruit, during my grasping around inside a darkness I now believe only years of net surfing will allow me to overcome, is the newsgroup alt.sex.stories. Here authors of works of erotica upload their masterpieces, some it would seem a first draft, most incomplete accompanied by a promise of more to come. The work can take the form of poetic verse, fiction, as well as first person narratives, and range in quality from excellent to.. well lets just say (and this is a quote from one internet citizen); "alt.sex.stories is like a box of chocolates." Many of the stories are noted along with their title, for the type of sexual acts they contain; ff (female and female acts), mf (male, female), mm-surreal, well you get the picture. There's even an anon service that allows you to upload your work to a newsGroup using an anonymous ID.

As far as the actual content of some of these pieces of fiction, I would not even be at liberty to begin to describe, using clean, wholesome words (if they existed), for some of the acts depicted in said stories.

An attempt was made by myself to contact by email some of the people responsible for uploading some of these stories to the groups, hoping to shed some light on their aim in posting these stories. My effort was in vein, and understandably so. The feeling one gets in accessing a lot of the alternative material on the net can be compared to walking through a pass frequented by prankish teenagers, where acts are committed not for any reason but for the fact that those acts CAN be committed. When it comes to the question of accountability, or even beginning to understand the merit of or intended end or reward in said act, there are few words.

Are you prepared for the new Pre-Armageddon?

It's 2002 and mankind is at war with itself. This is nothing new. War is not new to humankind. Nor are the drugs, decadence, violence and weapons of mass destruction, we now choke on like slimy, slithery mozzarella uniting in defiance, the pizza in your hands and a chewed remnant in the bottom of your alcohol polluted stomach. Excess and automatics are the order of the day, as you walk past the afternoon news on the big screen, past your kid at the terminal in the den, and her, inHome, onLine, brainBased education, on your way from your partTime, homeBased, business, to your afternoon jobShare.

Unemployment is sky-high. You're lucky to have a job. Working for yourself brings home some extra revenue, but mainly you do it cause you like it. Your business is in the service industry -you and ninety percent of the seventy percent of your neighbors that have started home-based businesses in the last few years. You provide Bob next door with a community newsletter, onLine. He collects your electronic mail, worldwide, and provides you access to it, onLine. The word onLine is as common and as delicious as the fish you've only last week allowed Amal, the grocer on your corner, to convince you to try. Fish as big and plump as any caught in a depth of the sea where the water can't help but be toxin free. But fish all the same reared by Amal in a tank the size of your TV, a tank in the back of his grocer. Salt water fish, engineered with the aid of a personal computer and software developed from data collected from years of ocean research, data downloaded in under two minutes from usc.silicon.edu in the directory; data/oceanography/fisheries.

On the way out the door the teleconference buzzes, vibrating in your trouser pocket. You ease the still open laptop to the ground, unwantingly taking the roll, the only food you've had all day, from your mouth. You ease the

vibrating contraption from your trouser pocket and flip it open, exposing your bosses face, pigified by the small console. He states no greeting. Only that he wants you in
that afternoon. Something about the girls having problems with the network. You say you can't. You were just out the door to your jobShare. You flip the annoyed look he gives you shut, and replace the roll. After all, you have an agreement with all your employers. If they need you, you need a day's notice. It's customary. You bend, securing the laptop, and you're out the door.

For as long as we have been fascinable, we have been fascinated with the future. Men far greater than myself have made forecast as to the future's contents. Pictures painted of the future fifty years ago, today seen as farfetched as the day they were published. The Jetsons and their panning bug in the sky are as far away as Vancouver, BC, and because of mountainous terrain, at least another day's bus ride away. With a new millennium less than four years away, something the supernatural have waited a thousand years for, the future seems a lot closer, at least in my too at times alcohol polluted mind. There is a sense that with this new dawn will come all of these things man for the last decade has dreamed of. Stun-rays, robots, hover crafts.

On the one hand, the automobile really hasn't changed much in the last fifty years. On the other, the last ten years has seen the evolution of what one day will surely be the answer to the question most commonly asked of students; "What is the most important invention ever."
Can you say cumpooder, boys and girls. The future will be full of innovation -Personal Telecommunication Devices. No not, the phone, video conferencing, pocket ones. OnLine you name it (A - Z). Reduced work hours, catch phrase of the year 2000 for unemployment. All brought to you by the word computing. The big question is, are you ready for Millennium 3.

Things come and go. Times change. Sure this is the norm. Happy? You might want to stop reading right here then.

Where there is change, people's lives are affected. When people don't anticipate this change, planning for it, they are run over by what might appear from behind, to any pulsating, pulverized remain, mammoth and asinine in scope. Those who have ignored the phenomenon of the personal computer to date will lay awake at night in regret. Those who refuse to see the giant inferno, growing like the thing that ate mankind, as it plunders, barreling, its path chosen only at whim, towards you, those who do not see the coming of the dawn, they will be ate alive as if by the aliens, whose unhygenic jowls we lie in wait of.

Millennium 3 will be a lot of things. It will not be compassionate. All will be there at arms length. But it will cost. Lots. Work, and for those of us that do not know, this is the staple by which one earns one's staple, will be delegated not permanently to an individual, that individual assuming this work will always be his to execute forever. Tasks will instead be contracted, and upon execution, the contract terminated. There will be no ties, no bonds, no benefits, and certainly no obligation. Only contracts. Those who assess need, and effectively satisfy that need, will likely do so independently. As this will probably become the norm, more and more of us pursuing this course, competition will be fierce. Those who cannot rise to the occasion, in possession of not one, but many skills and abilities, those who cannot command the very beast in the boiler room of destiny's engine, they will be consumed by it.

I'm J. Boooyah.

Tanarah Marlee

It's been almost two years since I became a father for the second time around. Little Tanarah Marlee.. was born Wednesday, October 11, 1995 at 3:48 in the morning. In my fatigue, I sat later that day in the middle of my apartment wondering about a lot of things, but wondering mostly about the future.. and about little Tanarah and her big sister Tarah's place in it.

Most of the pictures we paint of the future in our writing, and in our films and in our music, and theatre are pretty scary ones. I myself have already begun along that road to building a fortress around me and my loved ones. A fortress I need never leave, but will sit staring from the window of at the wasteland we envision below. Every time, I lose what little desire I have left, to walk the wild outside.. to mingle with others in the maze of our highways, for fear someone will cut me off, giving me the bird.. every time I dread the bustle of the crossTown bus to the downtown bound subway, fearing, knowing that somewhere along each and everyday day, someone will show me that degree of disrespect or ill-manners, that degree of inconsideration a fraction of a hair away from that which will cause me to totally lose it and spray them with the semi automatic I'm considering buying, every time I dread traveling to the mall to shop for very necessary things like food, every time I wish I didn't have to do these things, every time I think of more and more ways to eliminate these things from my life, every time I wish for shop at home supermarkets, is another 9 inch nail I drive in my front door.

What does the future hold for our children? Are we really going to sit in our dens, each of us, each family in isolation from the rest? Will our children really learn all that they need to learn about our world from a console? When they're old enough and they've ran off a copy of their online diploma on the laser, will they apply for a job online? And being successful, will they report to the console for their first day of work.. and their last.

Will they grow old looking from the window at the wasteland below, littered with bladeRunners and waterWorlds, hiding behind a UV protected glass window from the strange days below?

What does the future hold for little Tanarah Marlee?

:)

Aspire To New Bytes

Steak, removed from the freezer, has to sit at least half the day, preferably in the bottom half of the fridge and definitely in some kind of bowl or container of some sort. Try an empty cheese can. This can only add essance. Start in the morning as you step from the shower. On your way to cranking the machine, and that first crack at that much awaited email, likely not there yet, detour to the kitchen. Liberate yon steak from yon freezer and remove from packaging, placing in said bowl. Cover, Primordial! After you crank the machine, instead of standing there watching it count the RAM you already know you only have 4 megs of, leave the machine to its design, return to the kitchen, remove one large onion from the fridge, and proceed to peel and slice, (I personally like cross-sections), said union over top of steak, sitting in said cheese can. Cover! This is much needed flavor. If you've got soya sauce and cayenne pepper, splash and sprinkle respectively. Don't worry about the pepper. It's really not that hot. Sprinkle away. 'Sides, you haven't been maintaining proper levels of fibre anyway. Sprinkle a little more. A little bit of your favorite seasoning/garlic salt might help here. Now, if you don't mind sitting on the street car next to some gigababe of the opposite sex, (yes, that's right ladies, you can try this too), with your hands reeking of onions and garlic, stick them in, kneed the entire confection around yon cheese can. Really kneed this stuff into the meat. There's much flavor here. Much. Kneed! The tap you left running in the bathroom has probably caused the sink to over flow by now, so kindly return to the bathroom, promptly. Don't forget to cover the steak. Back in the bathroom, you can try to wash the smell from your fingers, but it won't work. Trust me. It won't.

Home from work? How was your day? Long? Feet hurt, huh, (if you're a programmer, interchange "feet" with "bum")? Don't worry, steak'll be ready in five minutes (more like twenty). Toss a pan on the flame. Doesn't matter what

one. Just toss one on. Pour just enough cooking oil to cover the bottom, (ladies, watching the weight, try a little agua). Secure another large onion from yon
fridge. Hey! I never said this was cheap. Let oil heat and cool some. Lower flame. Slice onion and one small cooking tomato, (if you're British; "tomato") directly into pan. If this is too uncivilized, too cretin like, slice it into a dish, then dump it into the pan. Add a splash of water. Much steam here. Cover. And let simmer, uuummh.. one minute! OK, go run a bath...
..Bath afoot? Great! At this point, I personally, with the aid of a cooking spoon, remove simmered onion and tomato slices, (mulch by now) from pan and place in a dish, we'll need it later. OK, secure steak, shake all the crud you kneaded in loose, and plop steak in pan. Remember beef needs many degrees of heat. Crank yon flame, and cover pan. Don't leave kitchen. It'll burn for sure. I cook both sides, at max flame, to a shade of brown I like, then lower flame to minimum. This allows steak to cook thoroughly, without crisping on the outside. Brush or plop a little pasta/barbecue/A1 sauce on upside, and spread tomatoes/onions mulch waiting in dish atop steak. Cover. Now you can leave kitchen, but not for long. Go check your email. Don't be too long though.

Mail's not there yet huh? Well, at least your steak is.

My steak I serve with a half a cucumber on the side. That's right. Cucumber. Half. A cucumber's a pickle before the salt and aging. I don't make wheels with it. Or rose petals. I don't gut it, slice it, dice it. I don't even peel the green bark from it. I just rinse it and cut it in half. Kuplunk. Half. With my sharpest Ginsu. My chop's diagonal of course, lest we forget style all together.

 By now my bath's been run. And it's me in the tub, steak on the side. If you fall asleep in yon tub, and don't get to finish your steak, don't fear. This is the best finger food you're ever gonna reach for, later when you boot up, jack in and go net warp.

Awalay

Awalay was referred to me by an associate. "You gotta check this guy's work out. It's Good" approximates the reference I was given.

I first met the man when he showed at my place to drop off some prints of the art. As I climbed to the bottom of the stairs to open the door, allowing him entry, I came face to face with this stealth fuMan cybertron, dripping with sweat from his hike to my downtown Toronto Pod from his. He'd never admit to being a cyberzen but, the figure standing facing me, removing fly shades, smoothing a fuMan do, could not, at least I was sure at the time, be anything but. He handed me a brown paper packet from the printers and I took it inviting him in, and removed the pics from the packet to peep them. He drank several long glasses of unlead, in a vain attempt to squelch the summer's swelt, before leaving. And without going into any great detail about my impressions after studying the work upon his departure, I'll let you make your own decisions.
(They're hard! Progressive. :)

The work, and an interview we conducted by phone weeks later, occupies the next couple of pages.

Q1.
Can you briefly describe the process of your art, from concept to completion?
A1.
I don't set out and do sketches of my work. The concepts for me, come together as I work.

Q2.
A lot of visual art is turning to the computer, in the way they're created and displayed. Is this something you do or plan to incorporate into your work?
A2.
No.

Q3.
There's a form of art that I like to refer to as "starTrek art". You know, the flowing brook that
appears to be a view from a window, but is really images in a video screen. What are your thoughts on this vision of "future art".
A3.
Well, I think some people can and will use this, I choose not to. As far as displaying my work with the aid of a computer, for instances having a show using computers, that's cool I have no problem with that.

Q4.
How do you see art in the next millennium.
A4.
I see art in the future like I see it now. The idea of using screens as a means of display, that's been around for a while. In the next five years computer assisted art, whether it be the development of, or the display of , will be very viable. I only see myself using the computer from a publicity standpoint.

..Q4. (Elaborated)
With respect to technology, the next big thing will be, not only making images appear three dimensionally, but making them interactive. This whole concept of everything being interactive, the idea behind what's been called, for the past number of years, a hologram, you know, virtual reality. That's the next step. Images won't just be 3D, they'll be in VR. And I'm sure art, or some peoples art will take advantage of this.

..Q5. (Elaborated)
Yeah, I can see myself using that, yeah. Cause again, it's your images that the computer is generating.

Q5.
Future art is usually in motion, free flowing parts and images. Is there any movement in your art?
A5.
No. But I see myself incorporating neon.

Q6.
What collaborative things do you do with other artists?
A6.
I'm working on a catalogue with another artist I did a show with last year.

Q7.
What are some venues where your art is displayed? Or what upcoming venues do you have in the works?
A7.
I've played in Yorkville, North York Board of Education, Metro Hall, just to name a few...I've got some things coming up, but no set date yet. Really, I've got a lot of things planned with other artists in this city -helping them to organize shows, doing a lot of talking trying to bring about a different mindset.
..There are certain things you have to do businessWise to achieve success. Artists have to stop being intimidated. We have to be able to mobilize. If you've got ideas, express them. If you expect opposition that's a part of conquering it.

Q8.
"What do you mean by Black is the XY"
A8.
Black is the biggest mystery. Many Blacks don't know themselves. And others don't know Blacks either.

WW3.. The War On Age _'Lyne Richard's Clinique De Beaute'

The year is 2013. The process of aging has been conquered. DNA, the code that defines when and how the years will affect one's appearance has been cracked. No longer will we have to grow old. No longer will a one die of natural causes. Immortality is here.. as long as you resist any urge to cross against red lights.

Ten years ago. Stopping the process of aging dead in its tracks was still a dream. I mean they were able to slow it, in some instances even able to alter its effects on one's appearance. With a visit to your local genetic scientist once a year, you could have your code reset from records kept of your last visit and, there you go, you've dropped a year's worth of age from your face, wrinkles from your body. Your doctor might have even pushed it two years, or three. Common sense dictated though. Since dropping a year in most cases created such a marked improvement, why push it. Why push science into those far reaches where you begin to lose data, where consistency seeps into invisible cracks creating inconsistency. A year is a great deal of age to have vanish from one's face. I do it every year on my birthday.

Now let's go back another ten years. It's February 1, 1993 and the grand opening of Lyne Richard's "Clinique de Beaute" in Yorkville, Toronto, Canada, the fourth of its kind in North America., with other locations in Montreal, Quebec City, and Boca Ratan, Florida. Now, the beginnings of the war on age are humble to say the least. There isn't this obsession with halting age, or reversing it. People, men and women alike are simply looking for content in their lives. The tone of the war is more along the lines of cosmetic enhancement, and cosmetic ease. Out of a need for maintaining ease in the application and maintenance of one's cosmetics, the idea of "permanent makeup" was born, not now in 1993 but some years earlier. One soldier though, because of a higher calling, an interest in beauty nurtured from a very young age, and a desire to elevate the state of the art, after 9 months of tutorship from pioneer Lyne Richard, a Quebec native, one soldier, Dorothy Kizoff set up shop in the upscale fashion quarters of Yorkville and never looked back. She specializes in what is called "Micro Pigment Implantation", a process of applying coloured mineral pigment beneath the skin. The process has many applications. There are the cosmetic purposes; permanent eyeliner, eyebrows, lipliner or lipcolor, highlighting facial features through the proper selection of pigment colors, to combat the signs of aging. And there are the corrective applications; camouflaging scars, birthmarks, and blemishes.

Business is good. People are thrilled at the idea of not having to apply makeup over and over, at the thought of never having smudged, running eyeliner, or smeared lipstick, never having to search through bottomless bags of cosmetics for the missing tweezers to pluck eyebrows. The procedure is not all that expensive; the eyeliner process running about $550. The clinic has a nurse on staff to apply anesthetic, and refers each client to a doctor for evaluation before the work is done. The tattoos aren't permanent either, lasting about five to seven years. And if someone is unhappy after the procedure, they can do it again, and have the look masked by flesh tone pigments.

About 40% of the work done in Toronto is in correcting skin abnormalities. But it is in the age defying processes, in the opinion of this writer, where there is the most promise. I'm not sure why, but I think some day, ten or twenty years from now this war on aging will be a really big deal.

Radio's Still Daa'h Man!!

Look'it. I've got hundreds of stations to choose from. If I leave town let's say in a rental even- for Datona Beach, Florida, as I move southwards my radio moves with me. Let's say I'm on the beach. I don't own a car so I'm jogging, or biking, blading.. maybe I'm in the middle of the ocean on a windsurf or a 50_ footer. Where e'er I go my radio goes with me. When they start wiring people up to receive stuff via their neuro.. whatdoya think you'll be tuning into first simply because of ease, simply because the framework's already there? Radio. Radiooo. RADIO. You can't beat it for selection. You can't beat it for size. And you can't beat it for price. It's free, Dolt!! Free. Freee. FREE! Well. Sorta. Heck you can even build your own. For the price of a ballPark hotDog, you can still score some transistors and other odds and ends and solder up your own. I haven't read a how to on the subject in a while. But I'm sure with our electronic revolution, the formula's changed in such a way that might make it even easier to build such devices. Grab some silicon from that obsolete 286 mother.. Our net is full of all kinds of info.. Surely there's something out there about building silicon chip radios. All you pre-teen gameHeads, and you reTeen net heads might do well returning to this a once proud pastime. Go ahead. Jackout. CyberPlace will be there when you return. Visit your local library. Dig through the rotting volumes. Find yourself something entitled; 'Build Your Own Transistor..' and go to it.

Think of it. What other medium gives you the ease of the radio?..... I'm waiting for reply. What other medium gives you the selection? What's that? Radio's too commercial. This why you lose yourself in the irreverence of the net. The net just sounds like college radio to me. 'Cept with college radio I get way, way more tunes and I'm not chained to some desk, starin' at some screen, waiting for traffic to clear.

TV. TV? Oh, TV!! You mean the tiny wrist ones they been

promising for thirty years. The portable ones they've only recently been able to ship. The little black and white, battery operated ones you can only get two channels on. That TV? TV's for losers!

Listen, if you're out cruizin' the strip, there's no alternative. If you and Sasha you met Friday night are planning a meet on the beach late Saturday night, and you wanna bring some entertainment along, there is no other choice. But if your name is Waldo, and the closest you ever come to a date is when you return your pocket calendar, stay home and watch TV tonight. Me and Jana we're going dirting, with radio head sets jammed over our lobes, and 'The Industrial Wasteland' (that's some radio programming, guess what about..) cranked to max. See you in a hundred years when the net's a lot more entertaining and they find a way to jack it to me while I'm on the go. Later. Much!

:)